A collection of

101

Poems

by
Gordon S. McCulloch

Cover: original artwork by
Gordon S. McCulloch

Table of Contents

FOREWORD

A fine collection of one hundred and one
poems compiled by Gordon S. McCulloch
covering a wide range of topics such as love,
romance, relationships, religion, prayers, the
meaning of life, death and our relationship
with God.
Some have been written in a manner that will
provoke your innermost emotions, while
others dig into the amusing side of life.
All have been composed under the auspices
of the Muse.

Enjoy.

I Stand

I stand in a corner out of sight
now that there's neither day or night
I am a shadow you cannot see
as you are now so once was me.

I stand in a place no mortal can see
I can touch you, but you can't touch me
I am a shadow of my former self
only because of the day I met death.

But I am not lonely
there's no need to cry
it makes me so angry
and ask myself why.

Here nothing can hurt me
so please, please do not cry
there are millions of others
like me also died.

As I wait in the corner
and I'm not here alone
there is somebody coming
to take us all home.

The Reckoning

I heard the footsteps at the door
that no one else could hear
it was an angel of the Lord
who suddenly appeared.

I heard the ticking of the clock
but time alas stood still
and knew that nothing I could do
could change that angel's will.

For time is but inevitable
it passes like the clouds
I saw that in the angel's hand
he held a snow-white shroud.

He beckoned me with smiling eyes
I did not hesitate
he told me I must come with him
as the light began to fade.

I saw the life that which I led
flash by me in a second
and all the rights and all the wrongs
for me would soon be reckoned.

Morning

The dewdrops sparkle in the morning air
as the sun begins to climb the heavenly stair
the unseen presence of God's artistic flair
begins to point this earthly solitaire.

And all alone in pensive mood I stray
as the argent river winds its weary way
across the open fields of new mown hay
and this all at the break of a new born day.

I would not but deny myself again
these very precious moments were well spent
among such beauty none can hire or rent
but only God through nature must have sent.

Divine Meeting

One day I saw an angel
looking down on me
she looked so sweet and beautiful
and that delighted me.

Don't ask me to describe her
for that I cannot do
for she appeared in front of me
as if from out the blue.

My eyes were they deceiving me
or was I over wrought
I've met a few wee devils
but angels not a lot.

She stretched her hands towards me
my heart it seemed to stop
and in a magic aura
the air around it popped.

She beckoned me come closer
and took me by the hand
it was a strange experience
I could not understand.

I was not disappointed
or was I filled with fear
as she whispered softly believe
believe and simply disappeared.

Forlorn

If you've never shed a tear
or if you've never cried
then something deep inside you
at one time must have died.

If you have never ever loved
or felt its tender touch
then something deep inside you
has hurt you very much.

If you have never ever laughed
or known the joy it brings
then something deep inside you
destroyed this wondrous thing.

If you could look outside yourself
instead of looking in
then something deep inside you
could help you to begin.

My Prayer

O God if you desert me
I don't know what I'd do
my life would be so empty
there's nothing else but you.

You are but the beginning
you are the ending too
there would be no creation
if it were not for you.

How beautiful my living
the end I'll leave to you
I do not ask for very much
the simple things will do.

I only ask forgiveness
for any wrong I've done
in the name of Jesus
your own begotten son.

This prayer is not for me alone
but every single one
who believes in the father
and Jesus Christ his son.

The Brothers

There were two lads I knew them well
and daring lads were they
they both had hearts, yes hearts of gold
and both had gentle ways.

One's name was John the other Jim
and both were twenty-two
but war broke out and off they went
to fight for me and you.

They landed on the battlefield
where shells like thunder roared
and watched their fellow soldiers die
as they tried to reach their goal.

Then up stood John and shouted
'charge, we'll win this battle yet'
but all in vain they plodded on
as shells and bullets rained.

The enemy had them in their sights
as John and Jim advanced
but neither of the daring lads
had but an ounce of chance.

A bullet struck John in the head
and Jim one in the chest
and down they fell, and in that hell
they did their very best.

The moral to this story is:
when your country goes to war
don't send you sons to use their guns
for they won't come back no more.

Confused Situation

I saw a figure in the night
all dressed in black and grey
I could not recognise the face
it was too far away.

The moon ascending in the night
peeped out behind a cloud
to cast the shadows of the night
spreading them around.

The figure moved from here to there
from one place to another
my heart it stopped my breathing too
I felt that I would smother.

A frightening sight on such a night
it made me agitated
I did not wait a second more
my legs began gyrating.

Who could that be on such a night
that figure black and grey
I could not tell you who it was
until this very day.

Panic

Last night as I lay on my pillow
a feather got stuck up my nose.

I cried to my mummy and daddy
and woke both of them from repose.

As both of them dashed to my bedroom
I could see they were wearing no clothes.

So I coughed and spluttered as they shouted
and the feather disappeared up my nose.

Power to the People

The King and Queen sat on the throne
with such majestic airs
a better pair was never loved
by all their subjects there.

With all the pomp and circumstance
such wealth you never seen
the very weight of all the stuff
was wearing down the Queen.

Their yes men stood around them
such sleekit men were they
to tell the truth I cannot lie
the most of them were gay.

The scandals that had reeked the court
should put the two to shame
for being of royal patronage
no finger pointed them.

They ruled their kingdom it was true
with such royal dignity
but they were blind to everything
especially poverty.

They spent their wealth upon themselves
their subjects they got none
and all the henchmen in their court
the public they had done.

The monies they were taking in
by tax and other sources
deprived the people of the state
to help with their resources.

But still the monarch could not see
the damage by corruption
among their subjects this would cause
a terrible eruption.

Kings and Monarch

How stupid are these silly fools
who think they are above it
when given power to rule the mass
into their face they shove it.

Though history is wrote by clever men
it sometimes makes me wonder
why it was writ with such esteem
by clowns that made such blunders.

I've read them all those stories tall
of rich men and the famous
and we poor souls take it in
and who you know can blame us.

What mighty battles have been won
by Kings and Royal Monarchs
not for the poor and poverised
'twas all inflicted on us.

How cruel those ancient people were
and that there's no denying
to have so many poor souls killed
and thousands just left dying.

The ancients tell such wondrous tales
of greatness and of plunders
but that is just their simple way
to keep the masses under.

The rich man he will always gain
no matter who must suffer
and use the poor man when he can
to make sure he can prosper.

Homecoming

O lonely the moorland
O lonely the sea
I dream of my darling
my loved one to be.

How dark are the mountains
how quite are the glens
time passes slowly
till we meet once again.

You're gone from the valley
and I'm left all alone
I dream of the day
when you're coming back home.

Till the day you return love
back home from the sea
I will wait forever
if ever it be.

Then we'll sit on the hillside
alone you and me
by our mountains and moorlands
overlooking the sea.

And we'll smile at each other
just happy to be
at home in the valley
at home you and me.

My Automatic Friend

For many years I had a watch
it sat upon my wrist.

I did not have to wind it up
but give my arm a twist.

I did not have to talk to it
nor did it talk to me.

But every time I looked at it
the time it told to me.

Foolish Things

Close to you I'd love to be
in your eyes what would I see
pools of gold or silver casks
these foolish things I'd never ask.

But in your arms I'd long to stay
and hold you O so tenderly
so close beside you let me stay
don't ever turn you love from me.

Then my darling by and by
off together we would fly
to our heaven in the sky
on a magic carpet you and I.

The Hunt

The earth was barren nothing grew
in the distance was heard the 'view halloo'.

As hoof beats thundered o'er the plain
a fox was on the run again.

Howling, yapping, barking dogs
had the scent of the frightened fox.

Men on horseback; men on foot
following in hot pursuit.

Then from the hill it was observed
as the hunter hunted, and the hunted swerved.

A gruelling race was near its end
the pack of hounds came round the bend.

The earth was red; the fox was dead
but not a single tear was shed.

Night

In the darkness when all is still
the frost creeps up my window sill.

And up above high in the sky
the moon smiles down as he passes by.

Black silhouettes of trees in the woods
stand out in the night like ghostly hoods.

The eyes of an owl watch out for its prey
and silently flies in the night until day.

The fox from its lair away it will go
to hunt for a rabbit or even a young roe.

Cubs playfully playing around the den
until it has brought home a kill once again.

In the quite of the evening when all is still
the frost from my window gives me a chill.

I get myself ready to go to my bed
and outside the world for me could be dead.

Gone to Hell

I died then left and went to heaven
when I arrived it was five to seven
and must confess it was not my scene
as everyone looked so spotlessly clean.

I had my doubts about this heaven
as everyone was pushing and shoving.

I decided then to go to hell
and must confess I could not tell
who was good or who was bad
but everyone was simply mad.

It's a place where one would never tire
as everyone helped stoke the fire
and in their hands they held a shovel
provided by Old Nick the devil.

A Knight's Errand

A knight went riding one day
'twas in the fair month of May.

He rode at speed on a snowy white steed
and his armour was silver and grey.

He rode with his sword by his side
had fought for his king far and wide.

But that day so they say
as he rode on his way.

He had hurried to be with his bride
but the saddle it slipped from the girth.

And he fell bodily to the earth
he landed in mud with a terrible thud.

And his horse, yes it bolted away
he struggled to get on his feet.

But the mud where he lay was too deep
try as he may he got stuck in that clay
and they say he is there to this day.

At Rest

She sat in her chair
and I could see
she was at rest
from the world and me.

Pale as a pearl brought
up from the sea
her skin was like wax
she was dead you see.

Time was no more
alas she was gone
to the place where they say
we need time no more.

She was my mother
I loved her you see
but we can't live forever
it's just not to be.

I will cherish those days
when she took care of me
from childhood to manhood
until she left me.

Aging

I saw her in the springtime
when first she took the air.

A bonny little rose bud
wrapped in her winter wear.

And then towards the summer
she spread her summer bloom.

She was a thing of beauty
but alas would fade too soon.

The autumn is the season
that turns the leaves to gold.

When all the things of beauty
with age alas grow old.

The Stolen Kiss

I stole a kiss from her sweet lips
I thought she'd never miss it
the kiss was such a tender one
I knew it was illicit.

I took the kiss and locked it up
and locked it in my heart
and from that day I must say
I loved it from the start.

She asked me to return the kiss
she said, please bring it back
I told her that I stole it
and locked it in my heart.

My dear she whispered softly
please give it back to me
and you can have another kiss
that isn't stole from me.

Confused

The more I think
I think the more
and what is more
I'm never bored.

The most of what
and what is more
I think that I
said that before.

The more I think
for I must say
I can't go on
like this all day.

I think I'll think
of it no more
I'll close my mind
and think no more.

The Leaves

The golden leaves of last year's summer
hue
lie heaped by roadways and on pavements
too.

The winter winds have stripped the trees all
bare
where green leaves once fluttered in the
summer air.

The buds of last year's spring are long since
dead
and now the remnants of their memories are
spread.

Upon the ground where once their mother
came
alas it's true to say they will return
again.

Desire

I made a wish at a wishing well
and hoped that it would bring
the secret of my heart's desire
fulfilling everything.

The wish I wished I wish it was
O no! I can't repeat it
for if I do it won't come true
and the fairies will redeem it.

The wish I wished will stay with me
I never will repeat it
and if perchance my wish comes true
my life will be completed.

Remember at a wishing well
when you wish for your heart's desire
you're knocking on the door of chance
and playing yes, with fire.

Satan

Across the earth he makes his mark
but don't you think it's just a lark
for he's no joke as you will see
the devil's not for teasing me.

He causes mayhem everywhere
with cruelty, hunger and despair
and you may help him here and there
better watch so please take care.

He has no shape or form you see
and that's the thing that bothers me
he creeps about and is unseen
he's weird and vicious and also mean.

He was disowned and thrown out
and that is what it's all about
he roams the world but has no face
and that is why he can't be traced.

Feelings

I cried so many bitter tears
that no one ever saw
and most of all to tell the truth
they never hurt at all.

For no one ever knows the hurt
in life that we endure
a broken heart is never seen
and that is true for sure.

A smile can hide so many hurts
to those we love so well
for they can't see the other side
that we can hide so well.

Deceive ourselves that's what we do
but time will find us out
deceit is only the facade
that turns us inside out.

Seasons

My roots are firmly in the ground
there's not but beauty all around
I see the seasons come and go
the wind about me always blows.

It was perchance that I did grow
upon the earth from seed you know
I bear some fruit among my leaves
and from their seeds new trees conceive.

I've seen the sky the colour blue
I've felt the cold of winter too
I've laughed and smiled in early spring
I've heard all types of songbirds sing.

And on my branches there will grow
the leaves of spring how green they show
through the summer I look tall
when autumn comes my leaves will fall.

Among my branches great and small
all kinds of insects hide and crawl
I never move my roots are deep
when winter comes I fall asleep.

Rain

Dull and grey across the way
I see the dark clouds gather
and in the distance not too far
the rain cries pitter-patter.

The river which for several weeks
flowed by as if lethargic
begins to flow at such a pace
and soon it may be tragic.

The power of nature we can't exceed
it can be so erratic
so don't be fooled by drops of rain
in mass they are dramatic.

For many souls have lost their lives
they said it did not matter
nor listen to the warning sign
as the rain cried pitter-patter.

Uncertainty

I came into this world and yet
I did not understand
the meaning of my purpose here
until I was a man.

The first few years upon the earth
I really don't remember
for I was but a little child
so delicate and tender.

All through my adolescent years
I got an education
to set me on a certain path
which helped with my vocation.

Alas, albeit, I must say
the world keeps changing every day
and in this life which we endure
there's nothing certain that's for sure.

Considered with some careful thought
the things in life that I have sought
were ill-timed or illusive; the roll in which
my life was filled was based upon conclusions.

Dreams

When to my bed to slumber go
all through the night but not to know
to dream of fantasies unreal
my soul from off my body peels.

Away, away, I cannot tell
exploring heaven or is it hell
I cannot keep myself intact
I'm split in two and that's a fact.

All through the night my body rests
but sometimes dreams are just a pest
I cannot tell how long they last
the dreams I dream are slow or fast.

What are those fantasies I see
when the dark envelops me
where are those places that I go
in the night when I slumber so.

Nature

Listen O can't you hear it
the wind that softly blows
across the golden meadows
where the wheat and barley grows.

Look O can't you see it
the sun high in the sky
shining down so brightly
as summertime is nigh.

O can't you hear the little brook
as it goes babbling by
inviting all the animals
to drink if they are dry.

O see the airy mountains
they tower high above
where nests the golden eagles
on ridges steep and rough.

O isn't it worth living
to see these wondrous things
when mother earth is happy
while mother nature sings.

Puppy Love

I met a maiden at the fair
a lass who took my fancy
I took her on the big cartwheel
she said her name was Nancy.

The pleasures that we shared that night
among the lights all flashing
and on the dodgem car she drove
I told her she was smashing.

She laughed at me and I could see
her heart was with me ever
that night of nights I'll ne'er forget
my heart was with her ever.

The crowds began to mill around
and things were getting chancy
O night of nights I'll ne'er forget
I lost my true love Nancy.

Night and Day

Night falls and no sound is heard
silently the clouds pass by
the moon hides its face
shrouded by a blanket of mist: 'tis cold.

Grey is the place in which I stand
the world is not asleep but wide awake
flowers by their predators are robbed
their colours are still there but unseen.

I wait and then alas 'tis morning
and a new fresh day is born.

The sun from the east is rising
and the shadows of the night flee
pursued by the light of the day
and I go on my way.

Guardian Angel

How sweet it is for me to know
that you are by my side
and every path of life I take
will be a pleasant ride.

How good to know that every road
may not be paved with gold
and every stop that I may make
I'll not stop there alone.

Though there be darkness on the way
I know that you'll be there
to care for me in every way
and hear my every prayer.

But if by chance the road may bend
and I from it may stray
help me please to right my way
before my dying day.

Mice

Under the floor boards of our house
is the nest of a timorous mouse
comfy, cosy, snug as can be
he lies there all day till it's time for his tea.

Then up comes the beggar
and searches about
like a thief in the night
who is looking for loot.

We cannot hear him
but we can tell
he's been in the pantry
and cupboards as well.

all through the night
he goes here and there
he leaves his deposit
of dirt everywhere.

Little black dots
that look just like rice
and that's how we know
in our house we have mice.

On Loan

Enjoy your life and contemplate
it soon will pass
and all too late you'll realise
how foolish that you were.

Enjoy the things that's given you
and all the things you own
for nothing in this life is yours
you have them just on loan.

Into this world you came alone
out from you mother's womb
enjoy yourself while you are here
your destiny's the tomb.

The Market Place

One day I came upon a place
a privilege to be
it was a hamlet old and quaint
surrounded by some trees.

Along the rustic street I went
up to the village square
a market was in progress
and everyone was there.

Some were buying some were selling
and some just browsed around
and others were delighted
with the bargain they had found.

There were cars and there were lorries
there were tractors there as well
the farmers brought their animals
in the hope that they would sell.

There were horses there were cattle
and many kinds of sheep
the people who were selling them
hoped they wouldn't sell too cheap.

The afternoon was hectic
at the little village square
I must confess to everyone
I'm glad that I was there.

The Christmas Tree

The Christmas tree at Christmas time
is such a pretty sight
it's filled with lots of ornaments
and pretty twinkling lights.

Adorned with lots of trinkets
for everyone to see
but underneath those glossy things
it's just a plain fir tree.

Little Star

O little star above me
all silver and serene
I know not where you come from
so I can only dream.

You twinkle in the evening
when the sky above is clear
and I never ever see you
when the clouds and mist appear.

O little star above me
I wonder what I'll do
I know I'll never see you
when the morning sky turns blue.

Will you be there still hiding
and keeping out of sight
when you know it won't be long
until the day turns into night.

Our Nanny

The night was dark and we could hear
the storm outside was raging
and every blast of wind that blew
it seemed to last for ages.

Be calm dear children don't be afraid
for nothing here can hurt you
the doors and windows are secure
and I am here to protect you.

The time drove on and it was late
the wind it blew much harder
the raindrops lashed the windowpanes
as if besieged by Tartars.

Be calm dear children don't be afraid
for nanny will protect you
there's nothing to be frightened of
the weather won't affect us.

Then all at once the doors blew in
the windows they were shattered
our nanny screamed and disappeared
'twas only her that mattered.

My Secret

I have a little secret place
where I can go and hide
where all my troubles disappear
when I simply climb inside.

It's not a very lavish place
most anyone could go
and if you want to know that place
I'll surely let you know.

It's upstairs in the bedroom
it lies upon the floor
a little piece of furniture
I simply just adore.

It's covered by a duvet
a pillow for my head
and if you haven't guessed by now
I'll tell you it's my bed.

Believe

What you believe in believe in it well
whether is heaven or whether its hell
whether its love or whether it hate
it's never too soon and it's never too late.

Believe what you like
it's all up to you
there's nothing to stop you
so do what you do.

But stop, look and listen
remember one thing
it's your life that you are living
so let your heart sing.

Remember the joys the good things can bring
when fish swim in the water it's easy to see
they never swim backwards
but forward you see.

So do what is right and you'll never go wrong
keep all things in place and where they belong
and you'll find that your life
will go by like a song.

Reflections

One day I stood beside myself
and wondered who I was
I had not much to think about
nor did I have the cause.

The emptiness surrounding me
was such a vacant place
until I came up close to me
and saw me face to face.

Who was this other side of me
I'll tell you I don't know
it must have been the other half
the one I used to know.

Then all at once I realised
that I was in a dither
the other half was really me
reflected in a mirror.

Mother and Child

Is it a girl or is it a boy
the midwife told her it's a bonny boy
the tears run down my mother's cheek
she was ecstatic and could not speak.

Then father came into the room
you could see by his face
he was over the moon.
I came into the world one morn
it was the day that I was born.

The midwife slapped me on the bum
I cried to the delight of my exhausted mum.
she wrapped me in a big white sheet
nice and cosy and all so neat.

Then place me gently on the bed
close to my mother's happy head
she kissed me softly then she said
it's time for my baby to be fed.

Man and Machine

I am not a machine
the machine works for me
I don't work for a machine.

The machine does not think
it is I who thinks for it
it is I who controls it.

Machines are built I was created
they don't have nervous breakdowns
they only break down.

Machine's wear and tear with time
I only grow old.

Machines end up in the scrap yard
I end up in the graveyard.

Machines can be recycled
I can be replaced.

Nightmares

I stood at the edge of a deep ravine
the deepest gorge I ever seen
and in the depths of great despair
I wondered how I ever was there.

But in a land where all is dreams
nothing is real, as real, it seams
for in the darkness I could see
vision filled with fantasies.

Visions which no hope is found
my feet were never on the ground
and in an instant I could be
any place I like you see.

I searched the canyons of my mind
when I left these dreams behind
I found that I could never find
the simple place called peace of mind.

Trivial

Good morning reverend
the young man said
it's a while since I saw you
I thought you were dead.

No-no I'm still living
and as you can see
my health is just fine
I'm as well as can be.

The young man just chuckled
and went on his way
I'm sorry to say
he died the next day.

Home Comforts

As I sit all alone by the fireside
I can see little flames dance around
like a troupe of professional dancers
and for music I don't hear a sound.

As I sit all alone by the fireside
I gaze at the beauty around
and enjoy all the little home comforts
in the home where all comforts are found.

The Candle

There's a candle in the chapel
and it shines for you and me
it burns there every evening
for everyone to see.

It's an emblem of a happening
that happened long ago
it's a light that shines eternal
and everyone should know.

When Jesus was a little child
a star shone from above
it was the light from heaven
that symbolised God's love.

Spring

The winter days had passed away
and spring came to the fore
then all the things that dormant lay
had come alive once more.

The sleepy little dormouse
peeped out to see the light
and ran among the bluebells
and snowdrops pearly white.

The crocus stayed a little while
for just a week or two
then told the golden daffodils
I must make room for you.

The daffodils just nodded
and told the tulips too
I'll make a golden blanket
the rest is up to you.

First and Last

Beyond the gates of paradise
one day I hope to be
to meet the people I had known
who went in front of me.

To share the joys of heavenly bliss
where Eden's garden lies
to see once more the friendly face
if people who pass by.

The sheer delight of such a sight
brings teardrops to my eyes
and though my thoughts are ever there
my heart's but one desire.

To live at peace with man and beast
upon this earthly planet
and hope that I will live content
until my days expire.

Homeless

I saw four chairs a standing
upon a kitchen floor
and near them was a table
beside the outside door.

But no one sat upon them
the table it was bare
the house it was deserted
and no one lived in there.

'Twas such an awful pity
the garden was ill kept
to someone who was homeless
it was hard just to accept.

But if you have no money
and you dearly need a house
to look from outside inwards
you'll never have a house.

For money is hard to come by
and it's easier to spend
so save it when you get it
you may find a house to rent.

Thoughtless

Today I had a thought
it was a simple thought
although I must confess
I do not think a lot.

First of all what was the thought
to think of it I don't recall
but in my mind I must say
I've thought a lot of thoughts today.

The memory is a wondrous thing
it fills the head with lots of thoughts
but what I've thought just then by chance
and to forget it's like a trance.

Alas the thought I do recall
it was not big nor was it small
I'm glad to say it came to mind
I thought I left my head behind.

Melting Moment

We met one day in winter
the snow was all around
'twas like a magic carpet
that covered all the ground.

You looked so cold and lonely
as the frost gleamed in your hair
there was a cold grey blanket
that shrouded everywhere.

Then all at once you smiled
as your eyes and mine did meet
the mists and snow just melted
and left summer at our feet.

Christmas joy

I'd love to have for Christmas
the things I've never had
a plum-pud they say is good
and a great big Christmas card.

I'd love to meet old Santa
they say he's a pleasant chap
but nobody ever told me
he's just my dear old dad.

So I'll wish you Merry Christmas
and also a happy new year
If I don't have a very good Christmas
you can bet I'll have a happy new year.

Sunrise

A jewel of the night
reflect your light
to guide me safely home.

A golden moon
you'll fade too soon
and I'll be all alone.

Though the darkness
may endure
I know it never lasts.

For day will break
and from the east
the sun will rise at last.

To chase the shadows
of the night
and keep my footsteps right.

Awe

Have you ever looked at life
and wonder how it is
that everything you see around
is not as real as is.

Some things are amazing
some things are filled with awe
the mystery of the whole dammed thing
they are not real at all.

Have you ever seen a face
that stands out in a crowd
then wonder where you've seen it
then start to think out loud.

Who were those passing strangers
you never seen before
you see them one time in your life
then don't see them no more.

Follies of Youth

When I was young and in my teens
my head was filled with romantic dreams
but of ambitions and what to do
remembering that I hadn't a clue.

Would I be rich or end up poor
like some terminal illness there was no cure
what foolish things went through my head
would I stay single or would I wed.

All through my youth
I had great expectations
and never understood
the word called patience.

Now I look back with deep regret
and sometimes ponder and sometimes fret
but age and wisdom is the cure
to soothe all things that is for sure.

Now I have plenty of time to spend
more time for me to understand
my youth was filled with discontent
but now in my old age I repent.

Once

The time has reached a crucial point
a time of no return
it is the age of innocence
the time for love and fun.

Enjoy the things
enjoyment brings.
and happy you will be
we blossom like a tree.

The crucial point has reached a time
when all the world is one
enjoy the moments of your youth
it only comes round once.

Little Leaf

I saw a leaf on yonder tree
its branches were all bare
but only one leaf did I see
determined to stay there.

The wind it blew with mighty gusts
but still the leaf hung on
Its branches seemed to lash about
but the little leaf was strong.

Then at the dawn one frosty morn
there lying on the ground
was the golden leaf that tried so hard
to stay the whole year round.

Dolt

What in my mind
these things conceived
a million thoughts
that I perceived.

My metal state
I can't control
tormented by
all things unknown.

I'm left perceiving
perchance perhaps
a million dreams
still wrapped.

Beyond contention
I concede
and go about
my daily deeds.

Imaginary

Where do fairies come from
please, O please tell me
are they just some spirits
roaming restlessly.

Sometimes in my garden
when all is quite you see
I hear little voices
coming from a tree.

Are they somewhere hiding
keeping out of sight
till the moon is climbing
among the stars at night.

Do you believe in fairies
just the same as me
does your imagination
sometimes set you free.

Waiting

No more your gentle voice I hear
you've gone away
I see those tears
that once ran down your cheeks.

I see them glistening
in the light
those watery diamonds of the night
that never turned to ice.

I see that smile you oft times smiled
that warmed a heart so dear
I see the face that once I held
in high esteem so clear.

But if a thousand years do pass
and I am left to roam
upon this earth in spirit form
I'll wait till you come home.

Nothing Ventured

Invidious that you might well be
scrupulous just your moral be
a man of character 'tis true
seamy others think of you.

Pretentious filled with aggravation
presumptions also over inflated
detached form overt palatial
everything seems trivial.

Belated all things overdue
nothing ever comes to you
waiting for something a new
life seems unreal so untrue.

Nothing ventured nothing gained
everything is just the same
try your hand at all you know
in the end there's not to show.

Life can simply be a drag
let it go and you will sag
manuscript the things you do
and you'll find you'll never loose.

Self Esteem

I swam in a pool of discontent
from one side to the other
although the surface seemed quite calm
it really was a struggle.

The pressures that were forced on me
to keep above the water
was ten percent above the line
the rest below the water.

I knew a man a pleasant chap
a gentleman by nature
but tortured was his very soul
and he himself beleaguered.

Judge not the things you see in life
or assault your aspirations
for nothing in this world is worth
the destruction of your egos.

Reflections

And now September has past by
the leaves have turned to yellow.

October is my birthday month
with age I'm growing mellow.

Across the years I now look back
look back across the ages.

As if my life were like a book
of chapters and of pages.

Each chapter reflecting what I've done
the course of life the pages.

The days pass by and so the months
and years they slowly age us.

We can look at each across the times
but can't reverse life's pages.

Dream World

I walked through the mist
of a dream last night
in a world I nearly forgot.

'Twas a time in my life
where I worked long ago
but nobody there did I know.

In the fog and mist
I wandered alone through places
I once used to go.

But time has passed on
and I'm here all alone
my body's not there you know.

For the time has passed by
and old friends have died
and I'm here in this world all forlorn.

Ambitions

A hundred years when you are gone
from this life to another
no one will know who you were
not even your own brother.

For all the things in life you did
will vanish without traces
the things you did
when you were young
and that when you were older
will live forever in your mind
but in the grave will smoulder.

For man is vain and in his quest
he strives to gain position
but little did he ever know
that was not his decision.

Presumptuous

She was a thing of beauty
that no one could deny
she was timorous and lovely
and also very shy.

She walked with an air of eloquence
her stature was divine
she knew that she was prudish
and her manners were refine.

A little bit presumptuous
she left pretence behind
but no one ever knew the things
that went on in her mind.

She had an in-built passion
she could not liberate
but woman being women
she left it all to fate.

But time it was her enemy
she did not realise
that age to every woman
is the thing which they despise.

Hope

I see reflections of my life
but all is not revealing
and castigate myself indeed
resolving all my feelings.

Berate myself that's what I'll do
beseech you to bestow on me
a kindness for my pleading
and I will live with no regrets
between us no hard feelings.

For life is but a carousel
with not too many pleasures
so if you find some happiness
then you have found a treasure.

Look not upon the dark side
for darkness is abundant
but hope you fill your heart with light
and all around you pleasure.

Where there is darkness
all is concealed
where there is light
all is revealed.

The Queen of Sleep

She sleeps upon a golden bed
a silver pillow for her head
a duvet soft is made of silk
her skin is pale and white as milk
she is a beauty lying there
the tresses of her jet-black hair
reflecting magic everywhere
her room is full of fantasy
she rests so peaceful I can see
have you guessed who this can be
she is the queen of sleep you see.

Time, Space and Distance

The distance between time and space
can sometime be breached
but no one can hold age back
nor hold time in their hands.

My Plea

Will you think of me
I know you will
in the evening
when winter chills.

Will you remember
when summers comes around
to pay me a visit
when I'm cold in the ground.

Will you stand above me
and say a small prayer
then whisper and say
forever you'll care.

Although I won't hear you
now we are worlds apart
in life as in death
we both knew in our hearts.

We were both passing strangers
who met for a while
we loved one another
and were married in style.

But the years pass so quickly
we just did not know
that each day that passes
the older we grow.

The door that had opened
to start life anew
had closed in behind me
that's why I left you.

Time Lost

Once in a single time
a moment gone forever
we met we spoke
and for a moment we were at one.

Alas, the time, the place had run its race
and that time was gone
O youth, why did you leave me
I know you had no choice.

Time is the enemy of all things
and cannot be defeated
age cannot be understood
for it is a dying process.

Once when in that single time
it was the time to be born,
to live, to love, to hate,
and to die.

To remember those times those moments
we lived, we shared in all these things
these memories will never die
but live eternally.

For like some deep-sea treasure
we all live in hope
that they will be retrieved again
maybe once in a single time.

Four Seasons

I've seen the clouds as they hurry by
but never saw the wind that sighed.

I've seen the spring bring things too life
I've seen the young man take a wife
I've seen his bride in pearly white
I've seen them both in sheer delight.

I've seen the summers hot and cold
I've seen the treasures it unfolds
I've seen a million colours too
I've seen the things it grew for you.

I've seen the autumn winding down
I've seen the leaves all turning brown
I've loved the seasons that came round
I've never seen the wind that frowned.

I've seen the birds in migrant flight
I've seen the days turn into night
I've felt the cold of wintertime
but never seen the wind in flight.

My Window

From my window I can see
all the things that pleases me
little things that don't mean much
the sky the earth my heart they touch.

I can see the seasons pass
the summer with the green green-grass
I see autumn turning brown
the leaves all lying on the ground.

I see winter pearly white
shrouding trees and things around
then when all these things have past
spring brings hope to me at last.

Aches and Pains

O dearest we are old now
and we have aches and pains
the simple things we used to do
are such and effort now.

I see the silver in your hair
the wrinkles on your brow
you see me fat and podgy
my head is egg shaped now.

My stomach's overloaded
it hangs with too much fat
and you always criticise me
for doing this or that.

But we are so contented
we sometimes have a chat
and talk about the neighbours
for doing this or that.

We are a perfect couple
there's no denying that
we have two dogs, two goldfish
and we also have a cat.

And outside in the garden
we also have two chairs
but we are far too old now
and cannot sit out there.

It's such an awful pity
with all these aches and pains
they're the only things in life dear
that both of us can share.

Spiritual Fantasies

Elves and fairies in the park
I often see them after dark
when I go there all alone
I sometimes bump into a gnome.

Happy little busy bees
seem to do just as they please
always dancing here and there
as if they didn't have a care.

When the moon is in the sky
I sometimes see the queen go by
what a wondrous sight to see
gnomes and fairies filled with glee.

I've been in the bar all day
drinking ale and malt whisky
and at night I lose my patience
that's when I have hallucinations.

I see all those things at night
when I'm drunk and don't feel right
in the morning when I'm sober
I'm so glad that it's all over.

So when you drink and like to frolic
you could end up an alcoholic
elves and fairies in the park
you could see them after dark.

The Storm

I heard the howling of the wind
that blew from east to west
me thought it was the devil
who was running out of breath.

The day began a pleasant one
as far as I could see
and in my mind the sea was kind
to all the crew and me.

We sailed two hundred miles from land
that cook had made the tea
when rumbling sounds cane from afar
he said what could that be.

The sky turned black and then to grey
then something troubled me
the waves began to rise and fall
to a height of forty-three.

The boards were strained to breaking point
and the crew could see
that if the storm got any worse
'twas death for them and me.

We turned for home and held our breath
and prayed that we'd be saved
we hoped that we would not be sent
down to a watery grave.

The turning point I'm glad to say
was when we sighted land
we thanked the Lord for guiding us
and for his helping hand.

Ignorance

Must I ask forgiveness
for everything I do.

Must I say I'm sorry
for everything I've done.

Must I apologise for the life
that I have run.

Must I keep my silence
for the things that I do.

Must I listen to those people
who say that right is wrong.

Must I be religious
because I'm told to do.

Must I listen to the crap
that people throw at me.

Must I die of ignorance
because I never knew.

Must I say with certainty
that all I say is true.

Wee Francy

Why is it when I think of you
my heart it seems to bleed
the sorrow that comes over me
my wholeness it concedes.

I knew you many years ago
when we were very young
two little boys with fantasies
and each with different dreams.

An age of innocence we procured
for we were best of pals
we shared in all our fantasies
and all our boyhood dreams.

But then one day
fate had its way
and took
my friend away.

Western Sky

O lonely island on the sea
my heart my soul are drawn to thee
where sea birds cry along your shore
I'd love to stay there ever more.

Beside your gentle silver streams
where I would wait and softly dream
of peace on earth forever more
O lonely island I adore.

By craggy rocks where puffins nest
the cormorant with is mate will rest
where razor bills and black bucked gulls
shelter when the sky turns dull.

To watch the fishing boats sail by
as the sun slowly sinks in the western sky
happy I'd be forever more
where the sea birds cry along the shore.

My Face

The face that I have is a wonderful thing
it can speak, it can smell, it can see
everything.

It can hear all the noises that were ever heard
and has plenty of room for me growing a
beard.

I know I'm no beauty so I have been told
but in summer and winter it can feel hot and
cold.

The face that I have is a wonderful thing
it allows me to eat and even to
sing.

I think I'll just keep it until I am dead
and hope it will always be attached to my
head.

Times Up

O prince of death your majesty
why do you come for me
I have not finished what I've done
so please O please leave me.

O no my son I cannot go
without you I've been told
you time is up so we must leave
you know you are too old.

O prince of death your majesty
where do you think I go
to that my son I can reply
you're going down below.

Modern Days

One day I saw a beggar
a coming to my door
he asked me sir please help me
for I have no place to go.

His coat it was in tatters
his face was cold and blue
he had no hat upon his head
and only had one shoe.

I asked him how he came to be
in such a dreadful state
he told me he had tripped and fell
while coming through the gate.

I asked him where he came from
to that he did not say
so I softly closed my door on him
and shouted go away.

Golden Moon

O Jewel of the night
reflect your light
and guide me safely home.

O golden moon you'll fade too soon
and I'll be all alone
but through the darkness may endure.

I know it never lasts
for day will break
and from the east the sun will rise at last.

To chase the shadows
of the night
and keep my footsteps right.

Regrets

I don't regret that night we met
'twas only for a moment
a moment sweet there at your feet
I left my poor heart bleeding.

Can you recall but after all
'twas just a simple meeting
that heart I left I still can hear
can hear it softly beating.

You

Because I found you in my life
you made this world for me
a heaven filled with ecstasy
a place worthwhile to be.

If only for a little time
we spent it both together
I won't forget I don't regret
the time we spent together.

For life is but a page of time
that can't be torn or tattered
and in that page are memories
for me that really matter.

Day to Day

You cannot walk into the past
nor go into the future
for you must live from day to day
and do the things that suit you.

Some people live and come what may
and never live from day to day
but live their life as one would say
in blindness filled with fantasies.

Reality is hard to bear
it's always with us it's always there
and each and every one must share
the daily tasks that we must bear.

Dawn

The morning sun shines bright
at the early dawn
the chill of night and darkness
all are gone.

The birds awake
and from their nests and fly away
and this all at the break
of a new born day.

The dew like gem stones
catch the sunlight rays
reflect the beauty
of another lovely summer's day.

And every plant and flower
that God has made
looks to the sky
as if in fervent prayer.

The Oak

There stands the oak tree in majestic pose
how long it's stood there no one knows
it is top heavy full of leaves
which flutter in the summer breeze.

Acorn fruit of this bold tree
soon will fall when they're ripe you see
squirrels will gather them for food
they know exactly when they should.

Hiding some beneath the ground
in larders when the winter comes around
some will lie there and sprout in spring
which brings new life to most everything.

Devious

A man stood by the counter
inside a family store
he asked for pipe tobacco
then turned towards the door.

'Excuse me sir?' a lady said
haven't I seen you here before
'indeed, you have,' was his reply
when coming through the door.

He stretched his hand towards her
her hands clasped his hands too
she was a young police officer
all dressed in navy blue.

You haven't paid for all your goods
but you have nothing on me
why don't you let me go.

I am a proper gentleman
and would never stoop so low
then turn out all your pockets sir
and let me see within.

I only have some whisky
some brandy and some gin.

The Dropout

One day I met a woman
who peered into my eye
I asked her where she came from
she pointed to the sky.

Was she just an alien
who came from outer space
and sent by some authority
to join the human race.

Or did she come from Glasgow
or was it just Milngavie
I did not look too long at her
to guess I would not try.

Her clothes were all in tatters
her hair was mat and dry
she only had one shoe on
upon her tiny feet.

And maybe lost the other one
while tramping through the streets
she had a funny accent
when she began to talk.

And was not very steady
when she began to walk
to me she seemed to mumble
and then just rant and rave.

I knew then it was vino
that she began to crave
she was a poor old dropout
who would end up in the grave.

Gypsy Love

By your camp fire burning bright
sitting by you through the night
gypsy dancers gypsy tunes
dance and play beneath the moon
dark eyes flashing bodies sway
dance and play the night away.

Love me gypsy love me more
I've never loved like this before
In the morning day will break
once again the world will wake
the sun will rise to spread its light
I will hold you O so tight.

Whisper softly tell me love
while there is a moon above
this is not a masquerade
you alone for me were made
I will love you all I can
beside your gypsy caravan.

Us

What lovely treasured memories
my dear I have of you
to think of all the things we did
together me and you.

Remember when the days were young
and we were younger too
we never thought that one fine day
we'd marry me and you.

We had our troubles more than enough
and always we pulled through
because we looked them in the eye
together me and you.

We had our squabbles yes many a one
and laughs we had them too
through thick or thin we knew we'd win
together me and you.

My Queen

So young and tender so supreme
of all the girls she was my queen
she was the apple of my eye
today I sit and wonder why.

But love is blind so I was told
and in my youth I was so bold
a beauty such as her I won
'twas then that married life began.

As time when by and quick it did
we got a house and had some kids
I worked my fingers to the bone
and nothing did I ever own.

The kids grew up and went their way
they came to visit at holidays
the wife is over sixteen stone
and likes a blether on the telephone.

As I look back across the years
the thoughts fill me with many tears
she hasn't time for me at all
although I'm old and getting bald.

The queen that once in youth I loved
has changed beyond redemption
the only pleasure I have now
Is going for my pension.

Childish Thoughts

If I could live my life again
I'd bring with me some money
I'd put it in a bank until
I was finished with my dummy.

I would not spend a single pound
although you'd think it funny
I'd live my life and be content
not worrying about money.

For if I know I have it
I'd be a millionaire
but then the bank I put it in
would I remember where.

Modesty

I am who I am that is me
I was born just to live and be free
not to be knocked around
or be even house bound
or to live like an ape up a tree.

I am proud of the things that I do
and sometimes I don't have a clue
but I try my utmost
without having to boast
and I know I'm as clever as you.

I don't have to prove what I am
and for me I don't give a damn
so take me or leave me
you won't ever grieve me
I won't live my life like a lamb.

Deserted

Alone the house is standing
nothing stirs within
the grass has now stopped growing
as winter coming in.

A cold wind blows so fiercely
now a chilling time begins
no light shines from the windows
as winters coming in.

We passed this way in summer
some children were at play
they were laughing they were singing
It was such a lovely day.

The sky it looked so beautiful
the garden it was too
the flowers they were blooming
and everything looked new.

Alone the house is standing
and nothing stirs within
It seems to be deserted now
as winters coming in.

The Rosebud

I saw her in the springtime
when first she took the air
a bonny little rosebud
wrapped in her winter ware.

And then towards the summer
she spread her summer bloom
she was a thing of beauty
but alas would fade too soon.

The autumn is the season
that turns the leaves to gold
and all the things of beauty
with age alas grow old.

Memories

Because I found you in my life
you made this world for me
a heaven filled with ecstasy
a place worthwhile to be.

If only for a little time
we spent it both together
I won't forget I don't regret
that time we spent together.

For life is but a page of time
that can't be torn or tattered
and in that page are memories
for me that really mattered.

Glossary

Big cartwheel - *Funfair ride.*
Blether – *Speak*
Blue halloo - *Urge on with loud shouts in a fox hunt.*
Glen - *Narrow sheltered valley.*
Lark - *Behave in a silly playful way.*
Ne'er - *Never.*
Nigh – *Near.*
O'er - *Over.*
Pest - *Someone who is annoying.*
Pitter patter - *A series of rapid tapping sounds.*
Plum-Pud - *Plum pudding.*
Poverised - *To be very poor.*
Reeked - *Smell strongly; stink, undesirable.*
Sleekit, - *Sly.*
Tartars - *Mongolian marauders who invaded Russia in the thirteen century.*
Tis - *It is.*
'Twas - *It was.*
Wee - *Small.*

Made in the USA
Middletown, DE
22 April 2021